THE POCKET GUIDE TO

ESSENTIAL KNOTS

For Jack, Becky, Charlie and Joe

THE POCKET GUIDE TO
ESSENTIAL KNOTS

A STEP-BY-STEP GUIDE TO THE MOST
IMPORTANT KNOTS FOR EVERYONE

PETER OWEN

Skyhorse Publishing

First published in the United Kingdom by Merlin Unwin Books Limited. This USA Edition of The Pocket Guide to Essential Knots is published by arrangement with Merlin Unwin Books Limited.

Copyright © 2020 by Merlin Unwin Books Limited.

First Skyhorse Publishing Edition 2020.

Skyhorse Publishing books may be purchased in bulk at special discounts for sales promotion, corporate gifts, fund-raising, or educational purposes. Special editions can also be created to specifications. For details, contact the Special Sales Department, Skyhorse Publishing, 307 West 36th Street, 11th Floor, New York, NY 10018 or info@skyhorsepublishing.com.

Skyhorse® and Skyhorse Publishing® are registered trademarks of Skyhorse Publishing, Inc.®, a Delaware corporation.

Visit our website at www.skyhorsepublishing.com.

10 9 8 7 6 5 4

Library of Congress Cataloging-in-Publication Data is available on file.

Cover design by Daniel Brount

Print ISBN: 978-1-5107-5222-1
E-Book ISBN: 978-1-5107-5223-8

Printed in China

CONTENTS

INTRODUCTION

It is an amazing fact that in today's high-tech world we can solve almost any problem via the internet or with some staggeringly clever gadget, but sometimes you still can't beat a good, old fashioned knot! People have been tying knots to solve problems since the beginning of recorded history.

Using a piece of rope, cord, string or twine and securing it with a knot is often a simple, practical and very comforting way to solve many everyday problems.

The Pocket Guide to Essential Knots will show you how to tie 21 key knots for everyday use: for home, work, hobby and play activities, indoors and outdoors.

This small handy pocket book does not pretend to be a knot encyclopedia, nor does it contain any knot-tying jargon or technical terms. It just contains easy to follow step-by-step tying instructions and possible uses for a handful of very useful and practical knots that should cope with most situations the average person will encounter.

Many people know how to tie one or two knots, not always correctly! This book is designed to give you a few more options. By helping you choose the right knot for the job and tie it correctly, this book hopefully will make life run just a little bit more smoothly.

KNOT-TYING MATERIAL

It is possible to tie a knot with an extremely wide variety of materials, both natural fibers and man-made synthetics. Natural fibers such as cotton, flax, jute, sisal, coir, hemp, raffia and manila are still used but in general they have given way to man-made synthetic materials such as nylon, polyester, polypropylene and polyethylene.

The essential knots featured in this book are most commonly tied with rope, cord, string and twine. Ropes are traditionally anything over 0.5inch (12mm) in diameter and are often referred to as lines. Smaller stuff is known as cordage; while strings and twines are generally even thinner.

Nylon, first produced in 1938 for domestic use, was the first man-made, synthetic material to be used. Since then wide ranges of artificial rope, cord, string and twine have been developed to meet different purposes. Size for size they are lighter, stronger and cheaper than their natural counterparts. They do not rot or shrink and are resistant to most chemicals and common solvents. They can also be manufactured in long lengths and a wide range of colors and patterns. Despite all of the advantages that man-made synthetics bring with them, there is of course still a place for natural fibers. For example nearly all gardeners take a massive pride in their gardens and want to do things right, not only in a visual and practical way but also increasingly in an environmentally friendly way. A piece of natural biodegradable twine which is soft, pliable and gentle to plants can, when finished with, be composted down—it never stops being useful!

Man-made synthetic rope, cord, string and twine do have some disadvantages, the main one being they can melt when heated. In certain circumstances even the friction generated when one rope rubs against another may be enough to cause damage, so if you use artificial ropes in this situation it is vital to check them regularly. Rope, both natural and synthetic, can be expensive, so it's worth looking after it properly. Always coil rope when not in use. If it is a natural fiber rope, always make sure it is dry before coiling and storing in dry conditions.

Correctly coiling a rope will ensure it will be immediately to hand when required.

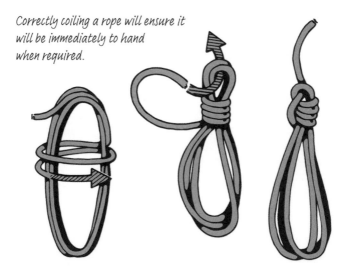

TYPES OF ROPE

Rope is generally divided into two types, **Laid** and **Braided**.

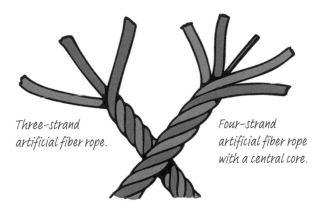

Three-strand artificial fiber rope.

Four-strand artificial fiber rope with a central core.

Laid Rope

Artificial rope can be twisted or laid like old-style natural fiber rope. Usually three strands of artificial fiber are twisted together to form a length of rope; this process can also be the same for cord, string or twine. One very strong variation of three strands is four strands of artificial fiber twisted around a central core of artificial fiber.

The cost of laid rope is generally about two-thirds that of the more widely used braided rope (see page 10). Laid rope, made of thick multifilaments tightly twisted together, may be resistant to wear, but it may also be difficult to handle because of its stiffness. As a general rule do not buy rope that is too stiff to handle.

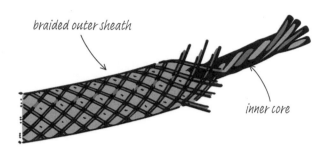

braided outer sheath

inner core

Braided Rope

The combination of an outer sheath surrounding an inner core makes braided rope softer, more flexible, and generally a lot stronger than other types of synthetic rope.

The outer sheath generally consists of 16 braided strands. This surrounds an inner core that can be parallel fibers, or twisted, or plaited. Both the sheath and the core contribute to the strength and flexibility of the rope. Its flexibility makes it ideal for knot tying, while the smoothness of the outer sheath makes the rope easy and comfortable to handle.

It is very often thought that braided rope is only manufactured in larger diameter sizes, but modern production technology also enables this highly successful material to be manufactured in very small diameter sizes.

How to Use This Book

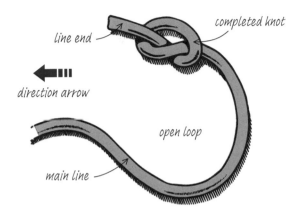

completed knot

line end

direction arrow

open loop

main line

This book makes a conscious effort to avoid any knot-tying jargon or technical terms—for example, the end of a line is simply called a line end.

The illustrations accompanying the tying instructions are intended to be self-explanatory, but additional written instructions are included at specific points. Arrows show the directions to push or pull and dotted lines indicate intermediate positions. In many of the illustrations, lines are shown faded out or cut short for clarity, plus a certain amount of artistic license has been used to enable the illustrations to fit into the available space. So always make sure you have sufficient line to complete the knot. This can often be calculated by looking at the illustration of the completed knot.

OVERHAND KNOT

This is the best-known and most widely used of all knots. It is also the simplest knot to tie. It forms the basis of many other knots and is often used in conjunction with other knots. The most common use for this knot is as a stopper knot at the end of a piece of thread, string, cord or rope.

① *Double the line to form a loop and then bring the line end over the main line and under the loop. Then pull out through the loop in the direction of the arrow.*

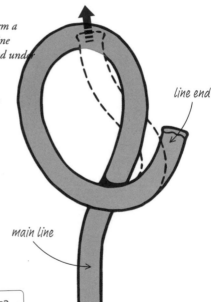

line end

main line

POSSIBLE USES?

• Tied at the end of a line to prevent fraying.
• To prevent a line slipping through a hole or eye.

+ A simple noose can be quickly formed using an overhand knot. A second overhand knot can be added to the end of the line to prevent the noose from slipping.

2 *Position the knot where it is required and then tighten the completed knot by pulling in the direction of the arrows.*

HEAVING LINE KNOT

The main use of this knot is to add weight to the end of a line, commonly used in sailing for throwing a line from boat to shore for tying up. Another name for this knot is the Monk's Knot as it is used to weight the ends of the cords they use as belts. It is a very versatile knot that can be used in any situation that requires a weighted end, a stopper knot or a grab point.

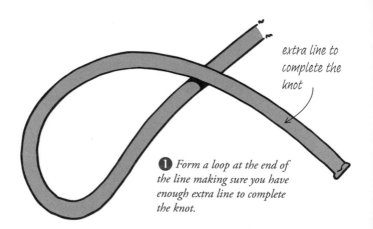

extra line to complete the knot

❶ *Form a loop at the end of the line making sure you have enough extra line to complete the knot.*

POSSIBLE USES?

• To add weight to the end of a line for throwing.
• To create the weighted end of a light switch cord.

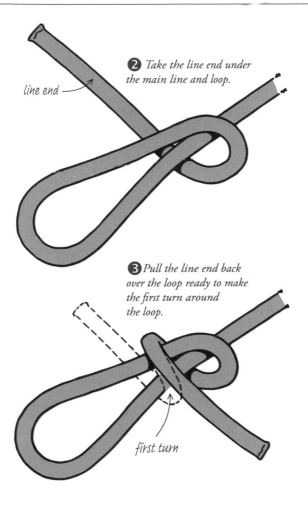

2 *Take the line end under the main line and loop.*

line end

3 *Pull the line end back over the loop ready to make the first turn around the loop.*

first turn

4 *Make four turns around the loop and on the fourth turn take the line end down through the loop. Keep the already formed turns as tight as possible.*

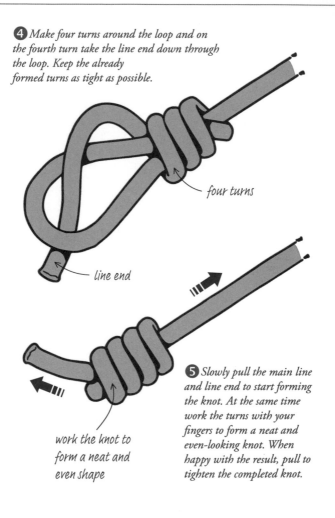

four turns

line end

work the knot to form a neat and even shape

5 *Slowly pull the main line and line end to start forming the knot. At the same time work the turns with your fingers to form a neat and even-looking knot. When happy with the result, pull to tighten the completed knot.*

REEF KNOT

The reef knot, or square knot, is one of the most widely known knots and is often the only one many people know. It is used to join together the ends of the same size string, cord or rope. It should only be used as a temporary join as it is not a secure knot and can work loose.

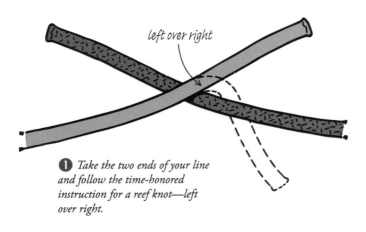

left over right

❶ *Take the two ends of your line and follow the time-honored instruction for a reef knot—left over right.*

POSSIBLE USES?

- Quick way to join two identical lines together.
- A comfortable flat knot tied in cloth.

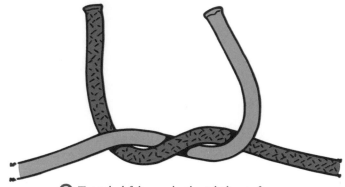

2 *Twist the left line under the right line to form the above, making sure you have enough extra line to complete the knot.*

right over left

3 *Take the two remaining ends and—right over left. Start to form the knot by pulling slowly and evenly on the two line ends and the two main line sections.*

4 *Tighten the final completed knot into its even and balanced form as above. If the knot is raised and uneven, you have tied a very unreliable Granny Knot, which is unfortunately a Reef Knot gone wrong, see below.*

granny knot

+ *The reef knot is an ideal knot for tying pieces of material together and is especially suited to bandages and slings.*

CONSTRICTOR KNOT

This is one of the best secure binding knots—it is a popular all-purpose knot that will grip tightly and stay tied. In fact, often the only way to release this knot is to cut it free. Specifically used for permanent fastenings, with the addition of a slip knot it can be released with a sharp pull.

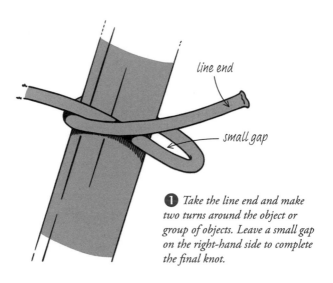

line end

small gap

❶ Take the line end and make two turns around the object or group of objects. Leave a small gap on the right-hand side to complete the final knot.

POSSIBLE USES?

- Securely closing the neck of sacks and bags.
- Securely binding together a bundle of objects.

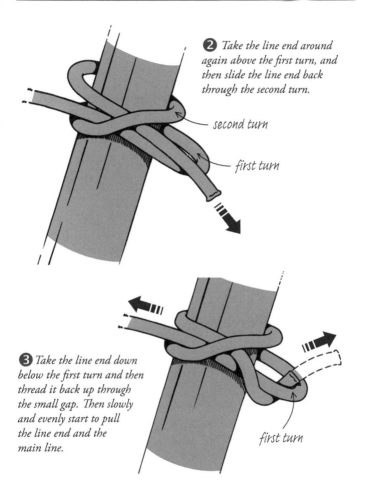

❷ Take the line end around again above the first turn, and then slide the line end back through the second turn.

second turn

first turn

❸ Take the line end down below the first turn and then thread it back up through the small gap. Then slowly and evenly start to pull the line end and the main line.

first turn

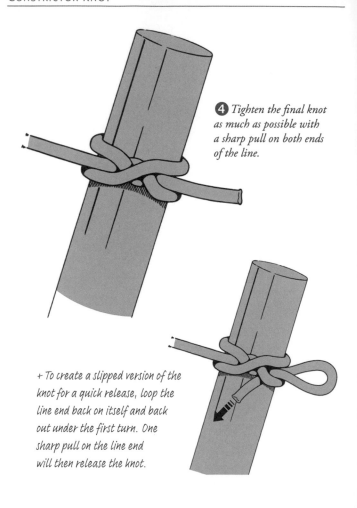

4 *Tighten the final knot as much as possible with a sharp pull on both ends of the line.*

+ *To create a slipped version of the knot for a quick release, loop the line end back on itself and back out under the first turn. One sharp pull on the line end will then release the knot.*

TRANSOM KNOT

This is an excellent knot for fixing together cross-pieces of wood, bamboo, canes etc., and often used in the garden for supports for plants. It can also be used in the outdoors for building shelters or temporary structures. While not as strong or rigid as a square lashing (see page 68) it is particularly useful for light jobs that require many knots to be tied.

first object

second object

❶ Pass the line around the first of the two objects to be secured and then back over itself.

POSSIBLE USES?

• Garden trellises, frames and plant supports.
• Temporary outdoor shelters and structures.

2 Pass the line end over the second object and back around the first object.

line end

3 Bring the line end around the first object and feed it up over the main line and through both of the turns.

main line

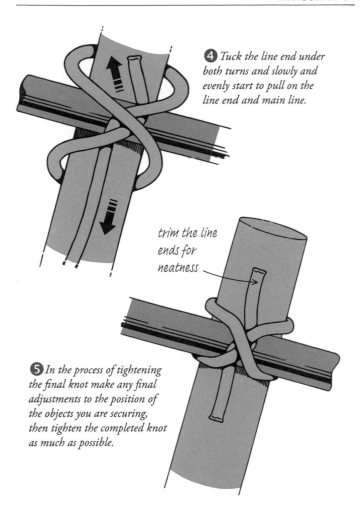

4 Tuck the line end under both turns and slowly and evenly start to pull on the line end and main line.

trim the line ends for neatness

5 In the process of tightening the final knot make any final adjustments to the position of the objects you are securing, then tighten the completed knot as much as possible.

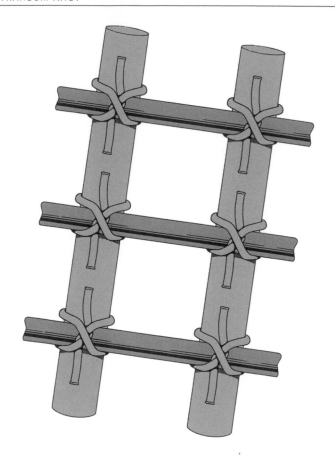

+ A wide range of structures can be built by joining together
cross-pieces of various material with a series of transom knots.

FIGURE-EIGHT LOOP

This is one of the best-known and most widely used loop knots. It is probably the safest and quickest way to form a fixed single loop at the end of a rope or line. A great endorsement of the strength and usefulness of this knot is the fact that it is often used by climbers to attach various pieces of climbing equipment, carabiners etc., to the end of a rope or line.

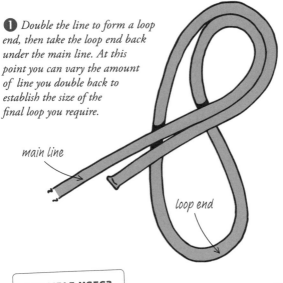

1 *Double the line to form a loop end, then take the loop end back under the main line. At this point you can vary the amount of line you double back to establish the size of the final loop you require.*

main line

loop end

POSSIBLE USES?

- A loop to place over or around an object.
- A loop to hold or pull an object.

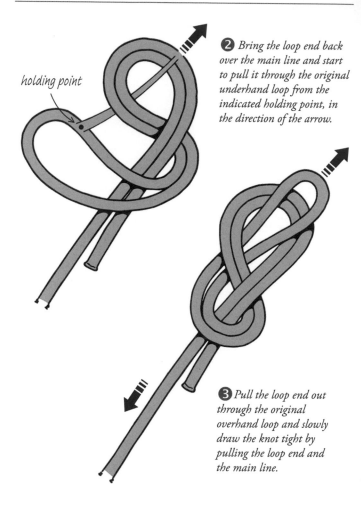

holding point

2 Bring the loop end back over the main line and start to pull it through the original underhand loop from the indicated holding point, in the direction of the arrow.

3 Pull the loop end out through the original overhand loop and slowly draw the knot tight by pulling the loop end and the main line.

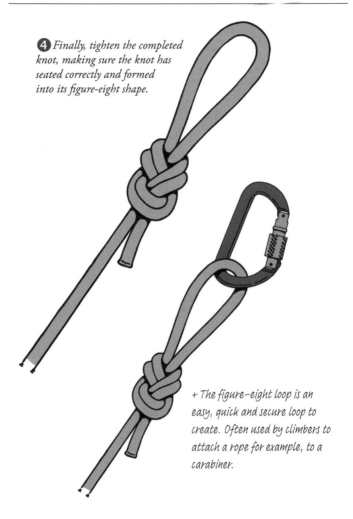

4 *Finally, tighten the completed knot, making sure the knot has seated correctly and formed into its figure-eight shape.*

+ The figure-eight loop is an easy, quick and secure loop to create. Often used by climbers to attach a rope for example, to a carabiner.

BOWLINE

The bowline (say *boh-linn*) is a practical everyday knot that is used to form a fixed loop at the end of a line or to attach a line to an object, for example when hoisting or dragging an object. It is a quick and easy knot to tie and untie. For added security the knot can be finished with a simple overhand stopper knot.

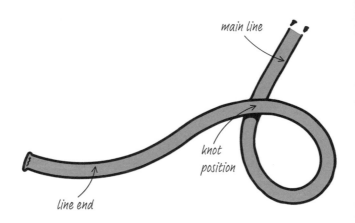

main line

knot position

line end

POSSIBLE USES?

· A fixed loop to hold and pull or drag an object.

· A fixed loop to place over or around an object.

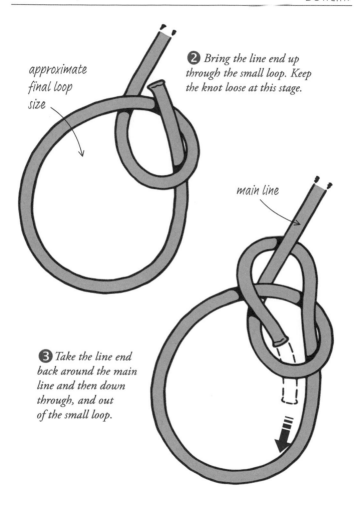

approximate
final loop
size

2 Bring the line end up through the small loop. Keep the knot loose at this stage.

main line

3 Take the line end back around the main line and then down through, and out of the small loop.

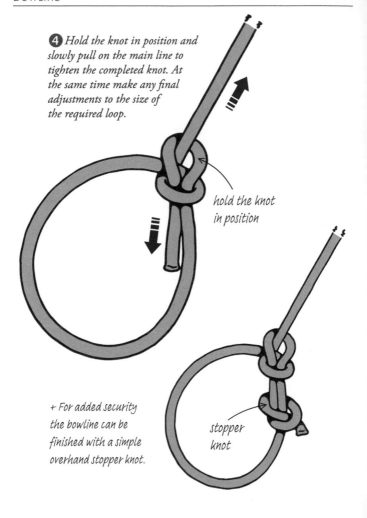

4 *Hold the knot in position and slowly pull on the main line to tighten the completed knot. At the same time make any final adjustments to the size of the required loop.*

hold the knot
in position

+ *For added security the bowline can be finished with a simple overhand stopper knot.*

stopper
knot

THREE-PART CROWN

This is an easy way to create a fixed double loop tied at the end of a rope or line. The two loops created are ideal for hanging objects with the advantage of varying the loop sizes for irregular objects. This knot can become difficult to untie after it has supported a heavy weight or object.

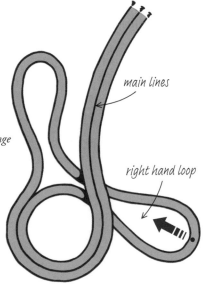

main lines

right hand loop

❶ *Double the line and then on a flat surface arrange the doubled line into this shape. Next take the right hand loop over the main lines as shown in step 2.*

POSSIBLE USES?

• A strong, sturdy knot to hang food or gear.
• A decorative knot to hang various objects.

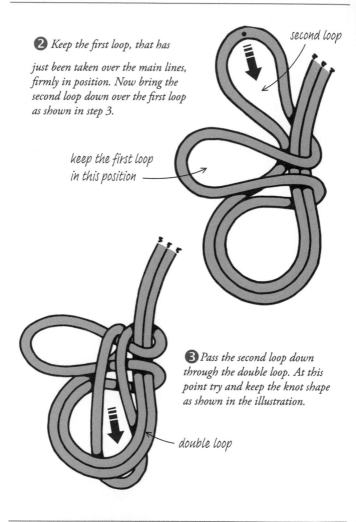

2 *Keep the first loop, that has just been taken over the main lines, firmly in position. Now bring the second loop down over the first loop as shown in step 3.*

second loop

keep the first loop
in this position

3 *Pass the second loop down through the double loop. At this point try and keep the knot shape as shown in the illustration.*

double loop

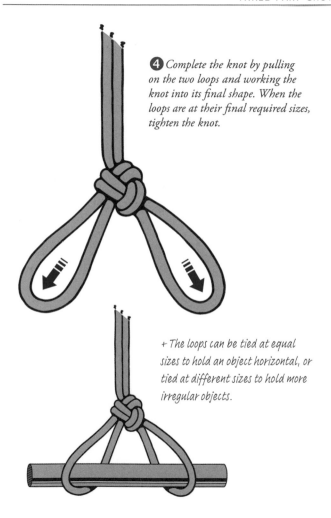

4 *Complete the knot by pulling on the two loops and working the knot into its final shape. When the loops are at their final required sizes, tighten the knot.*

+ The loops can be tied at equal sizes to hold an object horizontal, or tied at different sizes to hold more irregular objects.

Slip Knot

The term "slip knot" covers many knot variations. This version of the slip knot is very quick and easy to tie and can have multiple uses for temporarily securing objects. Once tied it can be drawn tight to secure an object or group of objects and then easily released to be used again.

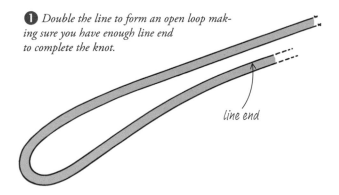

1 *Double the line to form an open loop making sure you have enough line end to complete the knot.*

line end

POSSIBLE USES?

• Temporary securing of object or group of objects.

• A quick attachment to a post or pole.

2 *Bring the line end back over itself, and the main line, to form a loop in the line end.*

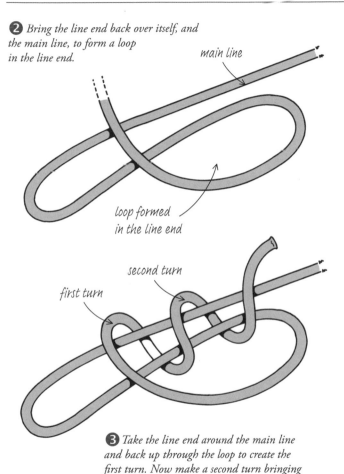

main line

loop formed
in the line end

second turn

first turn

3 *Take the line end around the main line and back up through the loop to create the first turn. Now make a second turn bringing the line end out through the loop.*

④ *Pull the line end and main line to start to form the knot. Slowly work and tighten the knot into its completed shape, making sure it can slide along the main line freely.*

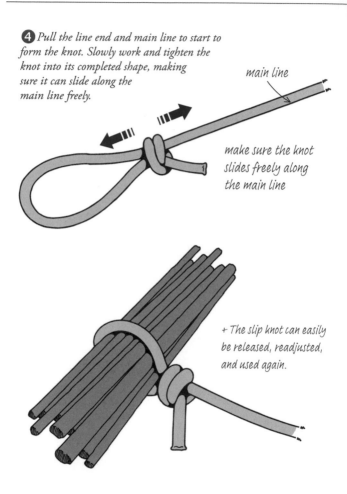

main line

make sure the knot slides freely along the main line

+ The slip knot can easily be released, readjusted, and used again.

Half Hitches

The half hitch is a widely used fastening with many variations and is often used to complete and strengthen other knots—as in the round turn and two half hitches (see page 42). The slipped half hitch is a very useful variation: one sharp pull on the end releases the knot.

❶ *A Single Half Hitch is a very simple knot. Take the line end through or around an object, back through the loop and pull on the main line.*

POSSIBLE USES?

· To strengthen or secure other knots.
· Temporary tethering of animals or objects.

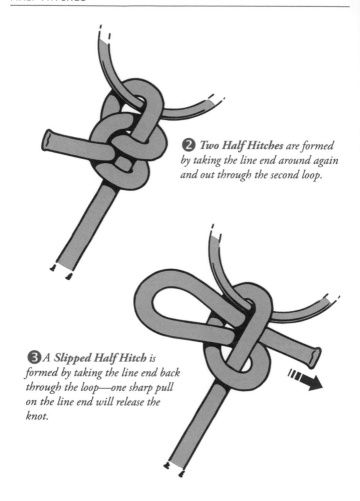

2 *Two Half Hitches* are formed by taking the line end around again and out through the second loop.

3 *A Slipped Half Hitch* is formed by taking the line end back through the loop—one sharp pull on the line end will release the knot.

Cow Hitch

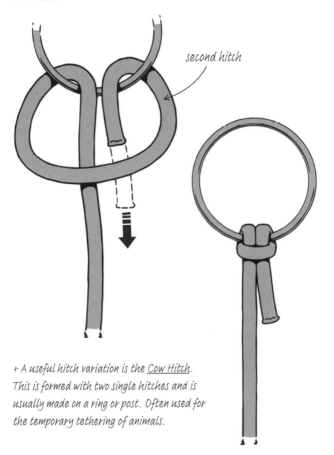

second hitch

+ A useful hitch variation is the <u>Cow Hitch</u>.
This is formed with two single hitches and is
usually made on a ring or post. Often used for
the temporary tethering of animals.

ROUND TURN & TWO HALF HITCHES

This very versatile, strong and dependable knot can be used for tying a line to a wide variety of objects including a ring, stake, post, pole, handle or rail. Once the end of a line has been secured with a round turn and two half hitches, the other end can be tied with a second knot, which is especially useful for fastening down unwieldy, bulky objects.

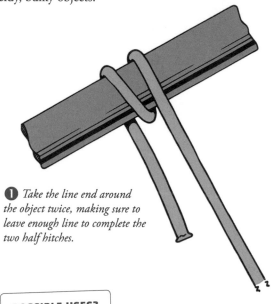

1 *Take the line end around the object twice, making sure to leave enough line to complete the two half hitches.*

POSSIBLE USES?

• *To quickly and securely attach a line.*
• *To tie down or secure a wide range of loads.*

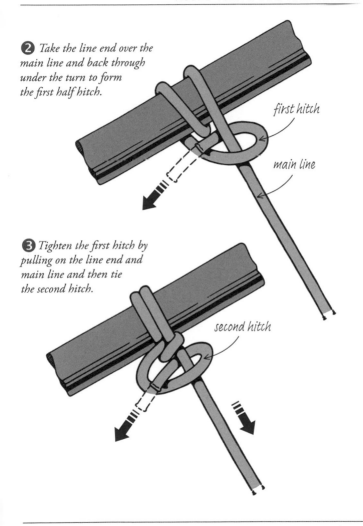

2 *Take the line end over the main line and back through under the turn to form the first half hitch.*

first hitch

main line

3 *Tighten the first hitch by pulling on the line end and main line and then tie the second hitch.*

second hitch

4 *Tighten the second hitch and then give a sharp pull on the main line to secure the completed knot.*

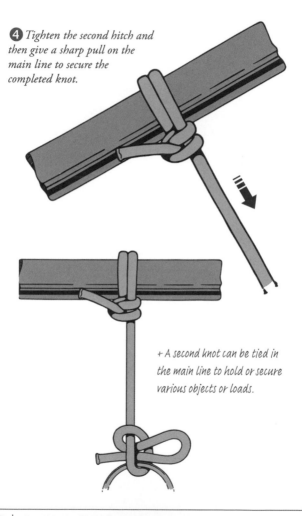

+ A second knot can be tied in the main line to hold or secure various objects or loads.

FISHERMAN'S KNOT

This simple but very strong knot is generally known as the fisherman's knot but is also known by a variety of other names including the English, halibut and waterman's knot. It is used for joining two lengths of similar diameter cord or line and is most effective with small diameter material such as string, twine and fishing line.

1 *Lay the two lines you want join parallel to each other and make a single overhand knot in one of the line ends, around the other line.*

single overhand knot

POSSIBLE USES?

• *Joining together two lines of equal diameter.*
• *Especially suited to small-diameter lines.*

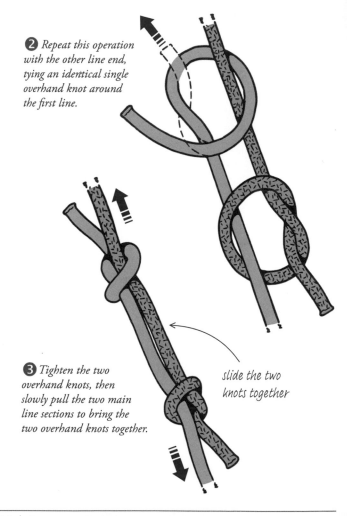

2 *Repeat this operation with the other line end, tying an identical single overhand knot around the first line.*

3 *Tighten the two overhand knots, then slowly pull the two main line sections to bring the two overhand knots together.*

slide the two knots together

4 *Continue pulling the two knots towards each other until they fit snugly together. Once together, pull hard on both main line sections to firmly jam the two knots together to form the completed knot and join.*

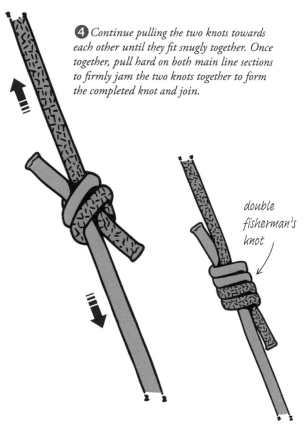

double
fisherman's
knot

+ To make the fisherman's knot even stronger and more robust you can tie the <u>double fisherman's knot</u>. Simply replace the single overhand knots with double overhand knots.

SHEET BEND

This is a good general utility knot for joining two lines, specifically if the two lines are of different diameter and material. It is quick and easy to tie, can withstand great strains, and is easily untied afterwards. The knot can also be modified quickly to create a "slipped" knot for quick release.

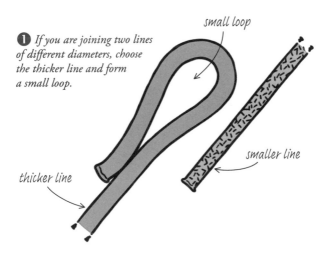

1 *If you are joining two lines of different diameters, choose the thicker line and form a small loop.*

small loop

smaller line

thicker line

POSSIBLE USES?

- Joining two lines of different diameters.
- A situation where a knot will be under great strain.

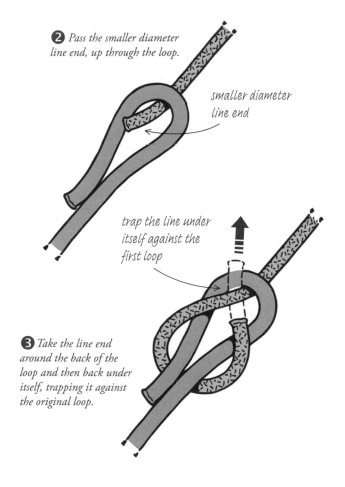

2 Pass the smaller diameter line end, up through the loop.

smaller diameter line end

trap the line under itself against the first loop

3 Take the line end around the back of the loop and then back under itself, trapping it against the original loop.

4 Tighten the completed knot by pulling on both lines. The strain will create the jamming action.

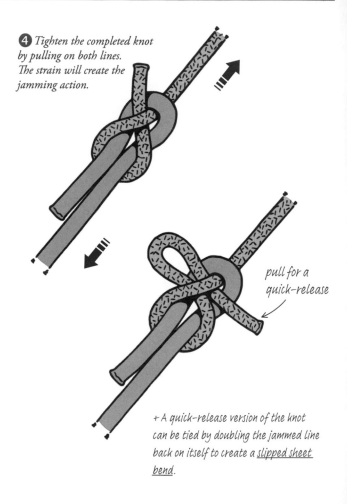

pull for a quick-release

+ A quick-release version of the knot can be tied by doubling the jammed line back on itself to create a <u>slipped sheet bend</u>.

PILE HITCH

The pile hitch is a very neat and practical knot for securing objects to a post—ideal for a temporary mooring of a small boat, but can be used with a variety of objects. The big advantage of this knot is that it is very easy to untie. Ease the pressure on the line and lift the knot off the top of the post.

❶ *Make a loop in the line and wrap it around the post.*

POSSIBLE USES?

· *Temporary mooring of a small boat or dinghy.*

· *Tying between posts to create a barrier.*

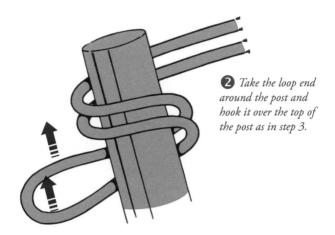

2 *Take the loop end around the post and hook it over the top of the post as in step 3.*

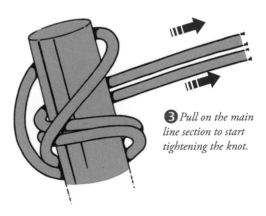

3 *Pull on the main line section to start tightening the knot.*

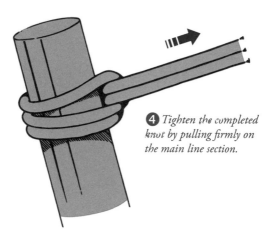

4 *Tighten the completed knot by pulling firmly on the main line section.*

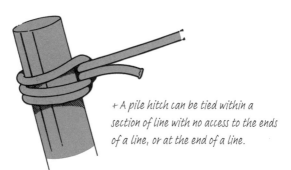

+ *A pile hitch can be tied within a section of line with no access to the ends of a line, or at the end of a line.*

CLOVE HITCH

This is one of the best known, easily remembered, and useful knots. It is used to fasten a line to a pole, post or ring. With practise this knot can be tied with one hand—useful when holding the object you are attaching to with the other hand. This is not a totally secure knot so best used as a temporary or decorative hold.

1 *Take the line around the object and underneath the main line. Bring it up to cross the main line, ready to pass around the object again.*

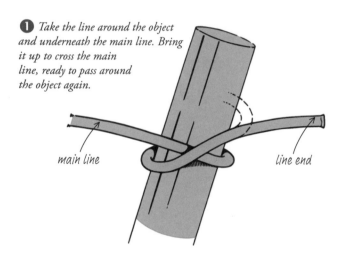

main line

line end

POSSIBLE USES?

• A quick way to attach a line to a pole or post.

• Making a temporary barrier or fence.

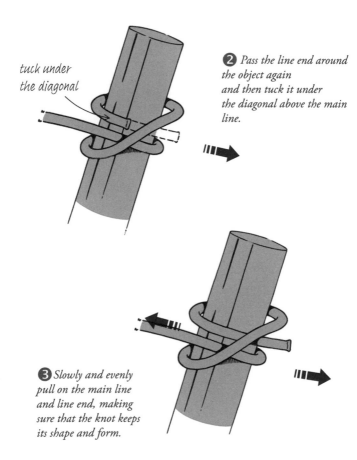

tuck under the diagonal

② *Pass the line end around the object again and then tuck it under the diagonal above the main line.*

③ *Slowly and evenly pull on the main line and line end, making sure that the knot keeps its shape and form.*

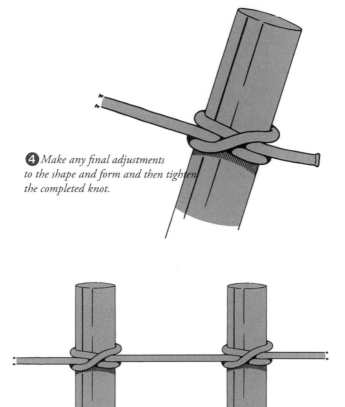

4 *Make any final adjustments to the shape and form and then tighten the completed knot.*

+ A clove hitch can be used to make a temporary barrier or fence.

Highwayman's Hitch

Allegedly named from its use by highwaymen, bandits and cowboys to give them quick release of their horses' reins and so ensure a fast getaway. The main part of the rope can be put under substantial tension, but one sharp pull on the rope end and the knot is released.

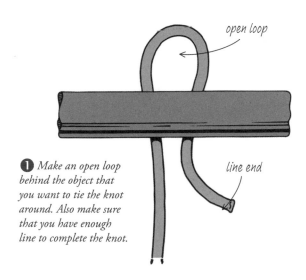

open loop

line end

1 *Make an open loop behind the object that you want to tie the knot around. Also make sure that you have enough line to complete the knot.*

POSSIBLE USES?

· *Temporary tethering of a dog or horse.*
· *Anything that requires a quick release.*

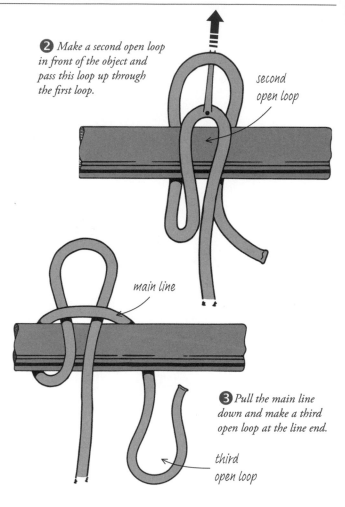

❷ *Make a second open loop in front of the object and pass this loop up through the first loop.*

second open loop

main line

❸ *Pull the main line down and make a third open loop at the line end.*

third open loop

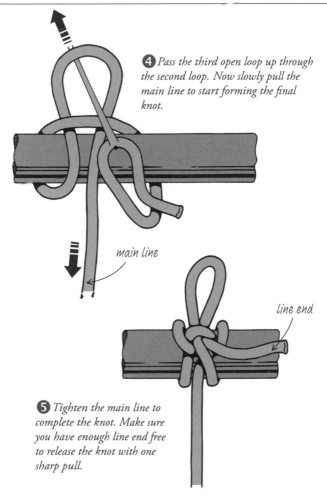

4 *Pass the third open loop up through the second loop. Now slowly pull the main line to start forming the final knot.*

main line

line end

5 *Tighten the main line to complete the knot. Make sure you have enough line end free to release the knot with one sharp pull.*

+ The addition of a longer
line end will give you the
option of releasing the knot
from a distance.

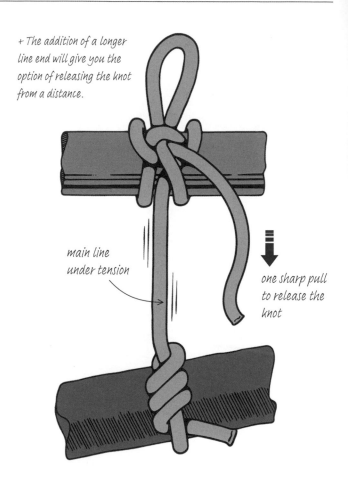

main line
under tension

one sharp pull
to release the
knot

Timber Hitch

This is a temporary hitch or noose formed around such objects as tree trunks, poles and planks so that they can be dragged or towed. It can also be used to raise or lower as long as the hitch is tied at the centre of gravity. The addition of a half hitch, which technically changes it to a Killick Hitch, allows for much more directional stability when dragging or towing.

1 *Pass the line around the object you want to secure. Then take the line end back around the main line and across itself.*

main line

line end

POSSIBLE USES?

• *To drag or tow tree trunks, poles or planks.*

• *To raise or lower objects.*

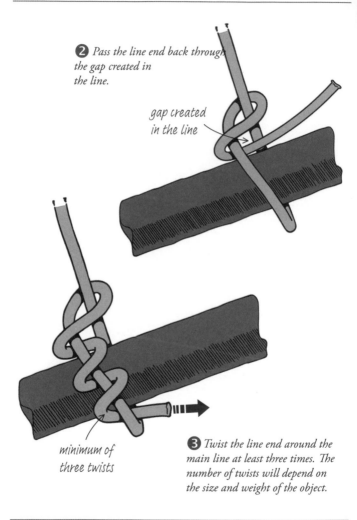

2 *Pass the line end back through the gap created in the line.*

gap created
in the line

minimum of
three twists

3 *Twist the line end around the main line at least three times. The number of twists will depend on the size and weight of the object.*

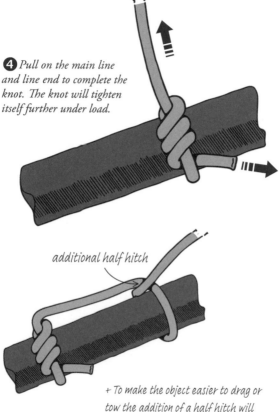

❹ *Pull on the main line and line end to complete the knot. The knot will tighten itself further under load.*

additional half hitch

+ To make the object easier to drag or tow the addition of a half hitch will help. This creates a variation of the timber hitch known as the <u>Killick Hitch</u>.

TRUCKER'S HITCH

This is a very practical knot that can be tensioned further after tightening the knot, making it very useful for securing objects or loads. When the knot has been fully tensioned, the line end can be secured to a securing device with at least two half hitches. Untying the half hitches will make the knot ready for immediate release.

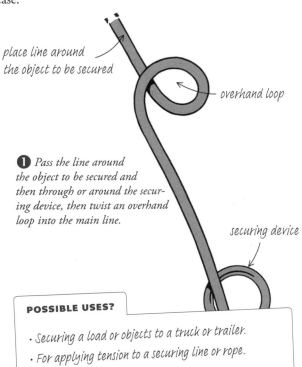

place line around the object to be secured

overhand loop

1 Pass the line around the object to be secured and then through or around the securing device, then twist an overhand loop into the main line.

securing device

POSSIBLE USES?

· Securing a load or objects to a truck or trailer.

· For applying tension to a securing line or rope.

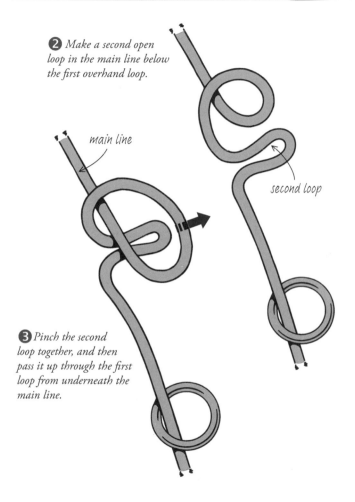

❷ *Make a second open loop in the main line below the first overhand loop.*

main line

second loop

❸ *Pinch the second loop together, and then pass it up through the first loop from underneath the main line.*

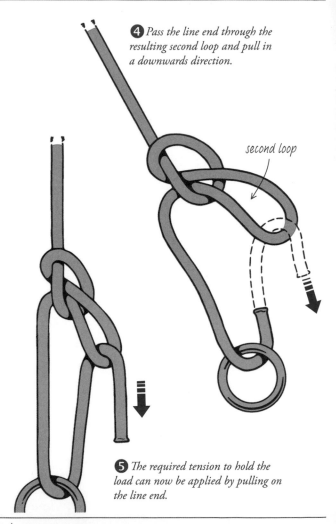

❹ *Pass the line end through the resulting second loop and pull in a downwards direction.*

second loop

❺ *The required tension to hold the load can now be applied by pulling on the line end.*

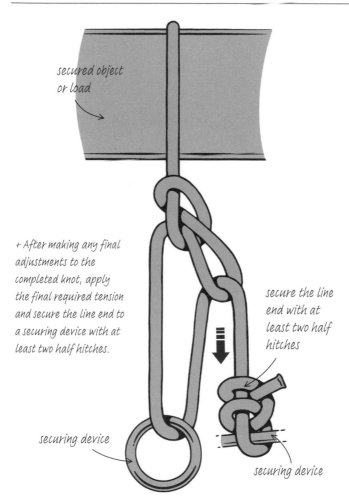

secured object or load

+ After making any final adjustments to the completed knot, apply the final required tension and secure the line end to a securing device with at least two half hitches.

secure the line end with at least two half hitches

securing device

securing device

SQUARE LASHING

Square Lashing is used to bind two poles together securely at a 90 degree angle. It is stronger and more permanent than the transom knot (see page 23) but takes longer to tie and uses more rope or cord. Square lashing is particularly useful for creating a rectangular frame or building a light framework.

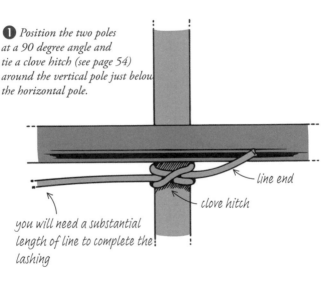

❶ *Position the two poles at a 90 degree angle and tie a clove hitch (see page 54) around the vertical pole just below the horizontal pole.*

← *line end*

← *clove hitch*

you will need a substantial length of line to complete the lashing

---

POSSIBLE USES?

· *Building light structural frameworks.*
· *Building garden trellis, arches or gazebos.*

2 *Pull the main line across to the right hand side and wind the line end around the main line. With additional windings this will hide and lock the line end securely.*

line end

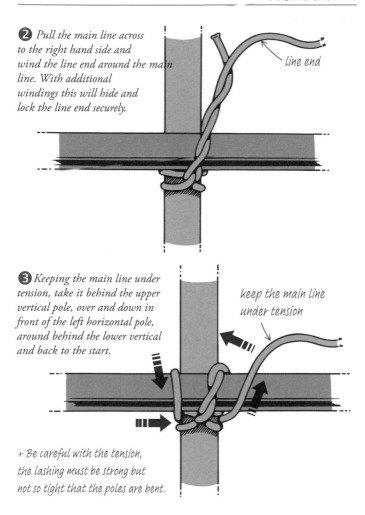

3 *Keeping the main line under tension, take it behind the upper vertical pole, over and down in front of the left horizontal pole, around behind the lower vertical and back to the start.*

keep the main line under tension

+ *Be careful with the tension, the lashing must be strong but not so tight that the poles are bent.*

4 *With the first winding complete, repeat the process about four times. The number of windings will depend on the diameter of the poles and thickness of the line.*

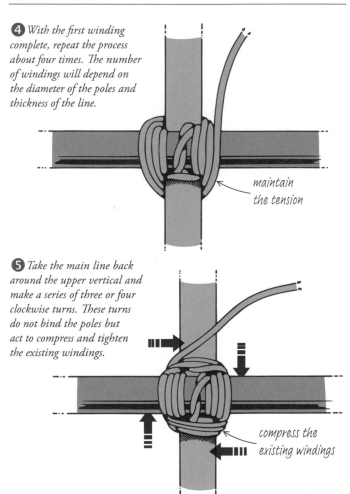

maintain the tension

5 *Take the main line back around the upper vertical and make a series of three or four clockwise turns. These turns do not bind the poles but act to compress and tighten the existing windings.*

compress the existing windings

6 *Stop the compression turns at the top left and complete the lashing with another clove hitch. This will stop the lashing from sliding or rotating under tension.*

trim the line end

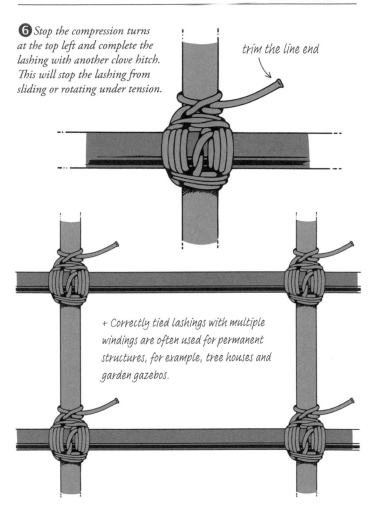

+ Correctly tied lashings with multiple windings are often used for permanent structures, for example, tree houses and garden gazebos.

DIAGONAL LASHING

Diagonal lashing is used to join two diagonal poles or spars that can be used to brace a rectangular frame. The two poles don't have to be at 90 degrees. The location of one diagonal in front and one behind explains the gap between the poles commonly found in the centre.

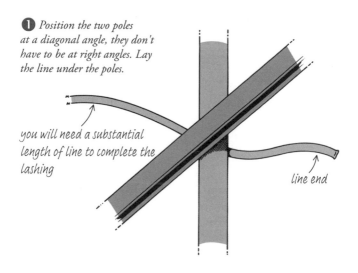

1 *Position the two poles at a diagonal angle, they don't have to be at right angles. Lay the line under the poles.*

you will need a substantial length of line to complete the lashing

line end

POSSIBLE USES?

• Securing poles or spars at odd angles.

• Building light structural frameworks.

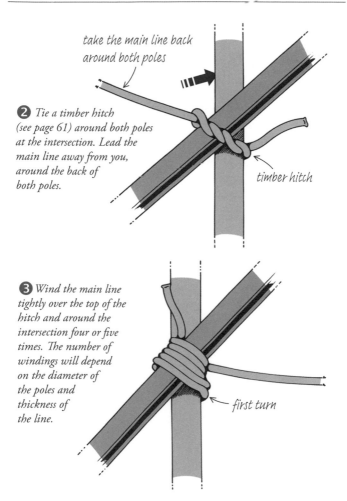

take the main line back
around both poles

2 Tie a timber hitch
(see page 61) around both poles
at the intersection. Lead the
main line away from you,
around the back of
both poles.

timber hitch

3 Wind the main line
tightly over the top of the
hitch and around the
intersection four or five
times. The number of
windings will depend
on the diameter of
the poles and
thickness of
the line.

first turn

4 *Now change direction and wind four or five times across the narrower intersection. This is the point that as you apply pressure to the windings you also set the angle you want to achieve. The line end can be hidden and locked within the next step.*

+ *set the angle at this point*

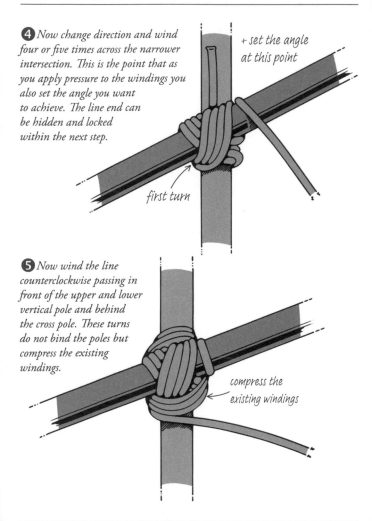

first turn

5 *Now wind the line counterclockwise passing in front of the upper and lower vertical pole and behind the cross pole. These turns do not bind the poles but compress the existing windings.*

compress the existing windings

6 Stop the compression turns and complete the lashing with a clove hitch (see page 54). This will stop the lashing from sliding or rotating under tension.

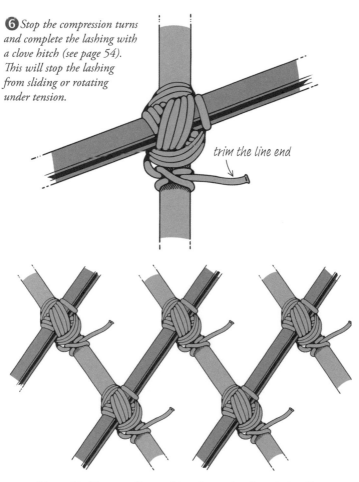

trim the line end

+ Diagonal lashings are often used to pull cross-bracing poles together.

TRIPOD LASHING

Tripod lashing joins three poles to one another for use as a tripod. There are various different forms of tripod lashing, but this version is particularly useful because it can tied into a frame, transported, and erected on-site. After use it can be folded flat and reused elsewhere. It could also, if required, be left as a permanent structure or part of a permanent structure.

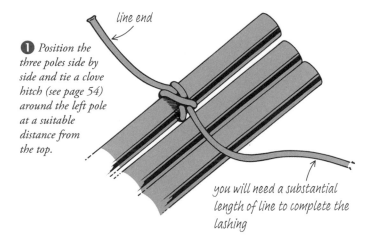

line end

1 *Position the three poles side by side and tie a clove hitch (see page 54) around the left pole at a suitable distance from the top.*

you will need a substantial length of line to complete the lashing

POSSIBLE USES?

· *Building a triangular garden framework.*
· *Support for suspending an object.*

2 *Wind the line end around the main line to hide and lock it and then lay the two across the three poles.*

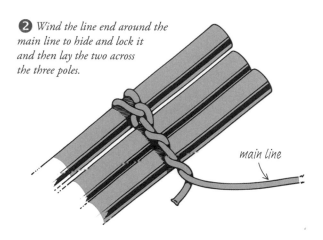

main line

3 *Start to wind the main line between the poles. Under the right pole, over the middle pole, under the left pole, then around and over to come back, this time under the middle pole, and over the right pole.*

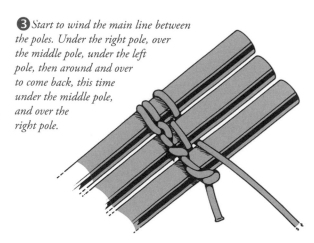

❹ *Continue the winding pattern for about five turns, the number of windings will depend on the diameter of the poles and thickness of the line. Stop the windings by bringing the main line out between the left and middle pole below the lashing.*

❺ *Now start to compress the windings by taking the main line up, behind the middle pole and down between the middle and right pole. Make a second set of turns in the opposite direction to the first.*

← *maintain the tension*

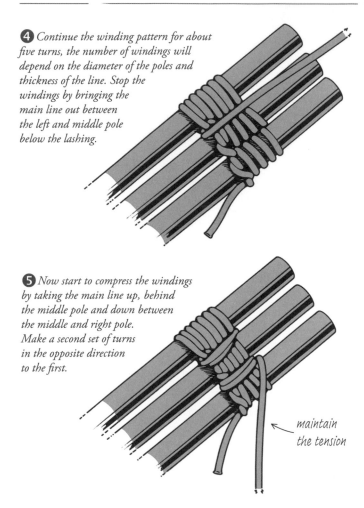

6 *Complete the lashing with another clove hitch. Make sure the final compression turn leads straight into the hitch, this will stop the turn from rotating.*

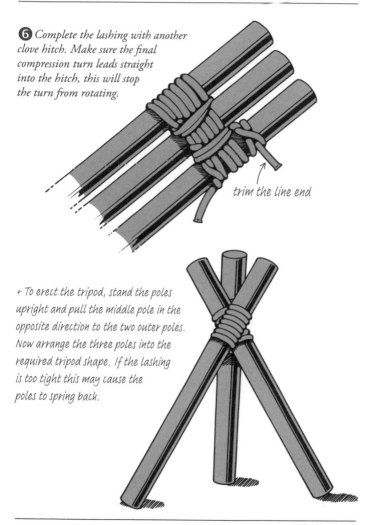

trim the line end

+ To erect the tripod, stand the poles upright and pull the middle pole in the opposite direction to the two outer poles. Now arrange the three poles into the required tripod shape. If the lashing is too tight this may cause the poles to spring back.

NOTES

Disclaimer

The author and publishers accept no responsibility for the manner in which rope or any other tying material and any knots featured in the book are used. The knot-tying instructions in this book are intended to help you learn how to tie the knots in a safe environment. Always proceed in a careful and cautious manner and seek qualified specialist advice from a professional before undertaking anything risky.